# Mom's the Word

**Attention: Schools and Businesses**

Andrews McMeel books are available at quantity discounts with bulk purchase for educational, business, or sales promotional use. For information, please write to: Special Sales Department, Andrews McMeel Publishing, 4520 Main Street, Kansas City, Missouri 64111.

# Mom's the Word

## More Momisms

CATHY HAMILTON

**Andrews McMeel
Publishing**

Kansas City

## "Don't interrupt me when I'm talking on the phone, unless you're bleeding on the carpet."

Mom's phone time is extremely important. The phone is the only way she can keep in touch with the outside adult world. It is her link with reality. Children would be well advised to stay clear of Mom when she's having a serious telephone conversation—especially when the subject is your middle-age neighbor's new young girlfriend.

## "The fastest way to a man's heart is through his stomach."

This ism, which is intended to motivate young women to learn how to cook, may seem like a throwback to the *Leave It to Beaver* era, but it still contains an ounce of truth today.

Of course, there is a faster way to get to some men's hearts, but Mom would never talk about *that* part of the body!

## "Have some more tea."

Tea is Mom's cure-all for every kind of ailment imaginable—from sore throats to stomachaches to heartbreaks—and the more tea, the better! Mom's thinking here is "If I can keep her mouth full drinking tea, she won't be able to moan so loudly!"

## "Nothing good comes from gossip."

This is Mom's valiant attempt to put a stop to insipid rumormongering. She will typically offer this nugget to kids *after* she eavesdrops on the latest dish about that hot quarterback and his cheating cheerleader girlfriend.

## "You look like a little angel!"

This is what Mom says when her child is:

a) all decked out for **church**;

b) **sleeping**;

c) actually dressed up like an **angel** for Halloween.

## "You never call, you never write . . ."

Here's a classic guilt inducer that simply means a child isn't keeping in contact with Mom frequently enough. "Never," in this case, could actually mean a mere two times per week, which, in Mom's mind, might as well be "never."

## "Men. Can't live with 'em, can't live without 'em."

Mothers send mixed messages about men to their daughters all the time. This one leaves a daughter completely clueless as to how to plan the rest of her life.

## "What do you mean 'What about Kid's Day?' Every day is Kid's Day around here!"

This is Mom about to lose it when she hears one of her children complain that they have Mother's Day and Father's Day, so why can't someone invent a Kid's Day?

(Especially when she has yet to pay off the Christmas bills.)

## "Wipe that stuff off your face. You look like a streetwalker."

Every adolescent girl is bound to make a few mistakes the first time she tries her hand at cosmetic application. This ism is Mom's not-so-genteel way of letting her know she's overdone it in the eyeliner and blush department.

## "Who do you think you are, the Queen of Sheba?"

This momism challenges not only a child's ego but her geographical knowledge. Most kids will hear this one and ask themselves, "What the heck is Sheba, some weird Third World country?"

# "Look me straight in the eye and say that."

Next to the polygraph machine, a mom is the most accurate lie detector on earth, especially if she can look her subject directly in the eye. Moms say this to ensure they catch every telltale twitch, sideways glance, and eyebrow furl, knowing full well that most kids will buckle under such intense maternal scrutiny.

## "Call when you get there!"

What she really means is "Call every twenty minutes until you get to your destination," but sometimes even Mom knows when to show restraint.

## "I'm getting too old for this."

This is what Mom says when, at her children's insistence, she climbs the ladder of the tree house to fetch an errant kite, embarks on a white-water rafting trip, or takes the plunge on the Tower of Terror.

## "Don't swallow watermelon seeds. You don't want melons growing in your stomach, do you?"

This ism falls under the category of "old wives" tale and, while it's difficult to believe that an otherwise intelligent woman would believe the possibility of enormous watermelon vines growing in a five-year-old's stomach, you can still hear this one uttered today.

# "You're beating a
# dead horse now, mister."

## TRANSLATION:

"You've asked for a new car six times a day for four consecutive weeks. The answer is still 'No' and if you ask me one more time, I'll see to it that you drive that old Pinto for the rest of your natural life."

## "Don't smoke!
## It will stunt your growth."

Moms have a long list of things that will theoretically stunt a child's growth, including cigarettes, chewing tobacco, coffee, alcohol, staying out after midnight, tattoo ink, and premarital sex. The better warning in this case might be: "Don't smoke. It'll stain your teeth and give you bad breath and then no one will ever want to kiss you! And besides, cigarettes are $4 a pack these days!"

## "What goes through the lips, ends up on the hips."

 Most moms are intimately familiar with this motto that cleverly warns against overeating.

This ism is used interchangeably with "I don't know why I bother eating this stuff. I ought to apply it directly to my thighs."

## "Are you getting enough to eat?"

When a child goes off to camp or college, one of the many overwhelming worries a mom has is if said child is going hungry. This makes absolutely no sense since the child has been using all of his resources to find food to eat since the day he was born.

## "I'm so mad at you I can't see straight!"

This is what Mom says when she's boiling, raging, over-the-top angry. It should not be taken literally, but if Mom happens to be driving when she screams these words, better encourage her to pull over . . . just in case.

## "Turn it down!
## I can't hear myself think!"

One of the many things kids don't understand is that when the music or TV is at a high volume, it drowns out the inner monologue running through Mom's head, which, at any given time, goes something like this:

"Don't forget to defrost tonight's dinner. Put the wash in the dryer. What was the name of that book Oprah was talking about? My nails need filing. The toilet needs scrubbing. Is that a varicose vein? Remember to pick up the dry-cleaning. What happened to the broom? Must schedule that mammogram. I hate my clothes. Who drank all the Diet Coke? . . ."

**Moms desperately need to hear this inner monologue or nothing will ever get done.**

## "Don't make me stop this car!"

In the chaos of the daily carpool, this ism should be considered a last-resort ultimatum. It's the red flag that should alert the young passengers that Mom is nearing her breaking point. Should she actually have to stop the car, God forbid, all hell is going to break loose right there in front of the Stop 'N' Shop.

## "Don't you know any normal boys?"

Mom's definition of normal: Clean, well dressed, gainfully employed, and college bound. Preferably the daughter's age but no more than two years older. Short, conservative hairstyle. No piercings or tattoos. Absent of leather except for letter jackets. Drives a conservative car. Well mannered. Comes to the front door on dates and converses with Mom with a well-rounded knowledge of business, current events, and sports.

This effectively eliminates 96 percent of all teenage boys.

## "So I saw you naked. So what? I used to diaper your bottom, remember?"

{ This is Mom's defense mechanism kicking into gear the first time she inadvertently walks in on her adolescent son stepping out of the shower and gets an earful, "Gawd, Mom! Can't you see I'm naked?!" }

### "My, how you've *grown*!"

This is what a mom says when she sees another mom's kid after a period of absence. Emphasis on the word "grown" occurs when the kid in question has transformed from a scrawny junior high nerd into a tall, strapping hottie reminiscent of those hunks on the covers of romance novels.

### "Not that it's any of my business, but . . ."

Warning! Warning! This maternal preamble means Mom is about to launch into an unsolicited soliloquy full of unadulterated advice.

## "You were the sweetest little baby. What happened?"

This momism makes an unfair comparison between the antics of a typical teenager whose hormones are raging and the behavior of a newborn baby whose days were spent sleeping, eating, and pooping.

When you think about it, the two really *aren't* that different from one another.

## "Don't spit!"

There are few things more horrifying to a mom than seeing her adorable little boy suddenly hawk a loogie on the street corner. As she spews out the above words, she is secretly thinking another ism, "You get that from your father."

## "God gave you half a brain. Use it!"

Now here's a rousing vote of confidence for you. What Mom really means is "Now c'mon. You don't really want my help with that calculus, do you?"

## "Your happiness is my happiness."

It's no secret that moms live vicariously through their kids.

---
TRANSLATIONS:
---

"Your '**A**' is my '**A**.'"

"Your first date is **my** first date."

"Your **promotion** is my promotion."

"Your **wedding** is my **wedding**."

"Your **first** child is my exclusive property."

## "Let's nip this in the bud right now!"

Moms love to nip things in the bud. Some moms could go around nipping all day if there were enough buds to nip. Among the things most nipable on Mom's list are cussing and other bad behaviors, budding young romance, and dreams of becoming a Vegas showgirl.

## "When is it going to be my turn?"

{ This isn't Mom impatiently waiting for a ride on a roller coaster. This is Mom asking a much bigger question: "When do I get to be the one who is cooked for, cleaned up after, and waited on hand and foot?" }

The answer, as we all know, is "Only when you're in bed with the flu, Mom, and probably not even then!"

## "Get a haircut,
## or I'll cut it for you!"

If there is a surefire way to motivate a son to get his hair cut, it's Mom threatening to cut it herself.

This one means "Better hightail it to the barber because I only know one style and it's called the 'bowl cut.'"

## "You'll get nothing and like it!"

{ The refrigerator is empty. Mom has scrounged the cupboards to come up with a dinner that could only be described as "Casserole a la Crapshoot." The kids are asking for dessert: "I want ice cream! I want chocolate cake! I want apple pie!" }

Nine times out of ten, their pleas
will be answered with the above ism.

## "All the 'sorrys' in the world won't help you now."

When a child is walking the plank toward a punishment so deep and long that he may never see daylight again, he will apologize profusely in a last-ditch effort to achieve amnesty.

This momism means "Save your breath. It ain't workin'."

## "Honey, we all have to go through it sometime."

{ Referring to those distasteful rites of passage like first dates, SAT tests, and trips to the gynecologist, this ism often offers little comfort to a suffering child. }

## "Put some ice on it."

{ Mom's first line of defense against injuries, cuts, and scrapes is ice. Ice numbs the pain, reduces swelling, and gives Mom a chance to steel herself before examining the disgusting wound at close range. }

## "Shoulda, woulda, coulda."

By the time most women become mothers, they will have identified approximately five hundred things they should have, would have, or could have done (e.g., earned their master's degree; auditioned for *Star Search*; had their tubes tied). That's why when they hear a child voicing the same kind of regret, they answer back with the above ism as if to say "I've heard it all before."

## "I'm serious!"

Sometimes, all a mom wants is to be taken seriously. But when she's standing at the foot of the stairs, wearing a lime green facial mask and bunny rabbit slippers, holding an armful of Beanie Babies, she's not all that convincing.

That's when it's necessary to make the above assertion.

## "What do you want to leave home for? You've got everything you need right here!"

In a desperate, last-ditch attempt to keep her baby bird from leaving the nest, Mom will say just about anything, including the above ism. What Mom doesn't realize, in this case, is that her baby bird really doesn't require her idea of "creature comforts" anymore. What he "needs" is unrestricted access to TV, a fridge, and all the women he can jam into his tiny studio apartment.

## "A lady never walks down the street with a cigarette!"

In *Mom's Big Book of Etiquette,* cigarette smoking in public ranks among the worst offenses, especially when one is on the street. Mom's concern here is not that her lovely daughter will resemble a common streetwalker but that people will think she's a bad mother who never reinforced the "Just Say No to Slutty Behavior" mantra.

## "What do I look like, a bank?"

{ A mom's job is to help provide for her family, balancing the budget so that there is enough money for all the necessities of life. A child's job is to obtain as much of that money as possible. }

That's why moms often feel like nothing more than an automatic bank teller . . . programmed to make nothing but withdrawals.

## "Do you have enough money?"

Mom might complain about how the kids are a constant drain on her wallet, but she'll be damned if any child of hers leaves the house with nothing in his pocket. That's why moms often slip twenty-dollar bills into their kids' hands before they go out for a night on the town.

And why they yell, "Be sure to bring back the change!"

## "It's what's on the inside that counts."

What she really means: "Okay, so she's no Britney Spears, but she's a nice girl with good values and there's no chance in hell of a shotgun wedding. Go out with her!"

## "You better have something to fall back on."

This tidbit of sage advice applies to college applications, career choices, and playing Superman on the top bunk bed.

## "Don't turn the air-conditioning on so high; you'll catch cold."

Here's another old wives' tale for which there is no medical support. In fact, scientists have proven through extensive research that air-conditioning, open windows, swimming in the ocean on a cloudy day, not wearing a light jacket, mixing Coke and aspirin, or playing badminton in your bare feet do *not* cause colds.

Just don't try telling a Mom that.

# "Rules are rules."

{ This is Mom's rebuttal when a debate-savvy child makes an indisputable argument against the logic, fairness, or legality of one of the laws she just laid down. }

---

TRANSLATION:

"You make a good argument,
but I'll be damned if I admit it."

## "If you can't say it in front of your grandmother, you shouldn't be saying it at all."

{ This little rule of thumb is intended to ward off cussing, off-color jokes, and other offensive language. }

It is usually effective, unless Grandma swears like a sailor.

## "Now I've heard everything!"

This is Mom's response when she hears one of her kids' creative excuses for staying out past curfew, such as: "We were on our way home from the party and spotted this van, full of nuns, stranded on the side of the highway. Well, we had to pull over and help them change their tires—all four of them! And it's a good thing we did because, at this moment, they're on their way back to their convent in Bolivia, just in time for the pope's arrival!"

## "Make sure you respect yourself in the morning."

Besides Aretha, nobody preaches about self-respect more than Mom. This ism is another way of saying, "The best way to start your day with self-respect is to wake up in your own bed. Alone!"

## "The older you get, the faster time flies."

This little tidbit of truth is Mom warning you to make each second count, live each day as if it will be your last, stop and smell the roses . . . and all that midlife crisis stuff.

## "You're getting so big!"

Mom takes delight in her developing child, eagerly marking growth spurts on the wall chart and applauding every inch. That is, until the child grows bigger than she is. Then this ism becomes less congratulatory and more ominous as Mom realizes she's looking up at the very thing she's trying to keep down.

## "You may be broke, but you're never poor."

{ This is Mom driving home the point that wealth isn't a matter of money. You can have zip for cash, but if you're rich in family and friends, you can feel like a king. }

Unfortunately, this point tends to be lost on the kid who just blew his gas money on a new video game.

## "Whatever it is,
## the answer is 'No.'"

Here's another one of Mom's preemptive strikes.
This one sends the following message, loud and
clear:

> "I'm in no mood for requests of any kind . . .
> and, chances are, it's all your fault."

## "I can teach you right from wrong but I can't live your life for you."

And thank goodness for that, because if Mom were living your life for you, it would be an endless string of cleaning, cooking, Sunday school, reading, and coupon clipping. In other words, you wouldn't be having *any* fun at all!

## "If I've told you once, I've told you a thousand times . . ."

This is Mom exaggerating. It was probably only a hundred times.

# "Pick a number from one to ten."

### TRANSLATION:

"I can't choose which one of you kids gets to ride the pony first because, no matter who I pick, I'll be accused of playing favorites. So we get to play this silly 'pick a number' game again."

# "Don't look a gift horse in the mouth."

---

## TRANSLATION:

"It doesn't matter where I bought you that Tommy Hilfiger ensemble. Ask me no questions, I'll tell you no lies."

## "Where'd I put my glasses (car keys, needle, drink, etc.)?"

Not so much a momism as a daily mantra, this question is commonly posed over thirty times a day. And the more kids Mom has, the more often she'll ask it. There is no hidden meaning here. Mom simply needs help. And fast!

## "Someday you'll thank me."

What she means: "I know you feel ridiculous right now but, believe me, when you're tripping the light fantastic with your bride on your wedding day, and your guests are oohing and ahhing at your Fred Astaire–like finesse, you're going to be glad I dragged you to ballroom dancing class when you were twelve."

## "Don't make a face.
## It might freeze like that!"

{ Deep down, moms know the likelihood of a face actually *freezing* in eyes-crossed-tongue-sticking-out mode is slim. But the mere possibility of it ruining all future family portraits is enough to prompt her to raise this red flag. }

## "Don't get your nose out of joint."

This somewhat outdated expression simply means "Don't get upset over trivial matters." It should not be taken literally as a nose cannot actually become disjointed from an emotional response, unless the poor kid throws himself into the door in despair.

## "Manners make the man."

What Mom is trying to avoid here is her lovely daughter getting involved with a guy who belches, farts, and scratches indiscriminately . . . just like her dad.

## "Don't forget
## to wash your hands!"

{ Any woman deserving of the title "Mom" knows that
hand washing is the best defense against any and all
forms of infection, disease, and overall offensiveness.
That's why she is constantly reminding kids and
inspecting their fingernails. }

## "Don't stick anything smaller than your elbow in your ears."

Intended to prevent trips to the emergency room for impaled Q-tips, pencils, and Barbie shoes, this ism often prompts little ones to actually try inserting their elbows in their ears, which can be highly entertaining, especially at cocktail hour.

## "Twenty* hours of labor for this?"

{ You know you're in serious trouble when Mom dredges up the old "hours of labor" routine. And you're in even *more* trouble if the number of hours in labor exceeds the number of times she's told you to pick up your clothes. }

*Substitute any number.

## "Have it your way."

Mom is being sarcastic now. What she means: "Why can't you see that *my* way is better than your way and just give in, for crying out loud?"

## "Go help your father."

Here's a clue that Mom is getting tired of her little ones "helping" her all the time. Why can't Dad share the love with a little "bonding time," preferably for several hours and miles away from home.

## "Let me tell you a little story . . ."

Uh-oh. When Mom opens with this ism, it means you're going to hear one of her special little fables, certain to conclude with an appropriate and instructive lesson.

The moral of this *story* is likely to be no fun at all.

## "You want something to do? I'll give you something to do!"

One of the first things a child must learn is never to approach Mom on a Saturday afternoon and complain that there's nothing to do. Chances are, she's got a list of chores a mile long in her pocket and she's just waiting for the opportunity to share the joy.

# "Can you hold it till we get home?"

Every day, mothers have to use a sophisticated mathematical formula to calculate the capacity of their children's bladders.

(**Example:** Emily is four years old and weighs forty-five pounds. She's consumed two six-ounce sippy cups full of apple juice in a one-hour period. How many miles can I drive at thirty-five miles per hour until Emily pees all over the backseat of my three-month old SUV?)

Sometimes, it's better to simply ask the child the above ism, then take them straight to a gas station anyway.

## "Nobody said it was going to be easy."

{ What she says: "Sure it's hard. The harder, the better. It wasn't easy for me or for your dad, and it's not going to be easy for you." }

WHAT SHE REALLY MEANS:
"If I could make it easier for you, I would."

## "You're always going to be my baby."

No matter how old, hairy, bald, pregnant, or wrinkled her children become, Mom will never forget that tiny, pink, sweet-smelling bundle of joy doctors handed her in the delivery room.

And she'll never stop reminding you of that very fact.

## "I just want you to be happy."

This is Mom's pat answer when she can't think of any other truthful responses to the following declarations:

"Mom, I've **decided** to enter a convent."

"Mom, I'm joining the **Navy**."

"Mom, remember that French girl you **thought** was a hooker? Well, we got **married** in Vegas."

## "Don't get up."

{ What she really means: "Get off your butt and help me with these damn groceries!" }

## "See what you have to look forward to?"

{ Spoken with more than a touch of sarcasm, this ism warns against the more mundane of adult chores like cleaning toilets, changing diapers, and taking out the trash. If Mom was to be believed, you'd think being a grown-up meant one endless string of stinky chores. }

## "As long as you tried your best, that's all that counts."

These words of consolation are meant to soothe the soul of a child who's just fallen off the balance beam, flunked a chemistry final, or come in dead last in a cross-country race.

This one is especially effective when followed by a hug, a kiss, and a double-scoop of ice cream on a waffle cone.

## "A penny saved
## is a penny earned."

This Ben Franklin gem is Mom making a gallant stab at a microeconomics lesson, though the logic is lost on most kids in the twenty-first century, half of whom don't know what a penny is.

## "Shape up or ship out."

You might hear this one if your mom runs an especially efficient household or grew up as a Navy brat. It is particularly obnoxious when punctuated by the high squeal of a sea captain's whistle.

## "Good things come to those who wait."

{ This timeless maxim is used by mothers all over the world in an attempt to encourage patience and postpone acts of personal gratification, like opening Christmas gifts, piercing ears, and premarital sex. It tends to get scant results but that doesn't keep moms from trying it. }

## "You expect me to believe that cock-and-bull story?"

Cock-and-bull story (n.): A tall tale. A lie. An alibi so far-fetched as to be laughable. Commonly used by teenagers caught with cigarettes in their purse ("I'm keeping them for Jessica so she won't get grounded") or coming home after curfew ("We all decided to go to midnight Mass").

# "Not until you're married!"

### TRANSLATION:

"No premarital sex. No premarital cohabitation.
No premarital pregnancies."

And if Mom is very strict: "No premarital dating!"

## "Oh no, that's okay.
## I'll do it myself."

This is one of the most effective guilt inducers preferred by moms ten to one over other tactics. It is a prime example of reverse psychology with a 95 percent rate of return in getting family members to pitch in and help.

## "Where does it hurt?"

In order to make an accurate diagnosis, Dr. Mom first needs to ascertain the origin of the pain. That will help her determine the course of treatment required, namely: ice, medication, or popsicles.

## "We'll see."

Here's another one of Mom's famous stall tactics intended to postpone the answer to a request for so long that the kid forgets what it was he so desperately wanted.

# "Don't be such a worry wart."

_____

## TRANSLATION:

"Worrying is *my* job. I'm extremely proficient at it and I'm doing enough of it for everyone!"

## "What you need is a nice, hot bath."

{ The hot bath is another one of Mom's cure-alls for what ails you—a sore back, damaged ego, or an inflamed heart. }

**NOTE:**
That's why when Mom finds it necessary to take a nice, hot bath, give her a little extra TLC. She obviously needs it.

# "I give and I give and I give some more."

{ When you hear Mom make this declaration, it's time for a significant "Thanks for all you've done" gift, such as flowers, candy, or a certificate for dinner for two at a five-star restaurant. }

### CAUTION:
An appliance of any sort is *not* a thank-you gift!

## "Where did I go wrong?"

{ When a child does something unruly, illegal, or out of control, no matter if said child is fifty years old and has been out of the house for thirty-two years, a mom will still blame herself. }

That's just the way it is.

## "The fresh air will do you good."

Fresh air is Mom's one-size-fits-all remedy for everything that ails you. Don't be fooled when you hear this one, because Mom knows that the one thing that will do *her* the most good is if everyone else in the house went outside for some fresh air.

## "Santa Claus doesn't bring presents to boys and girls who don't clean their rooms."

One of the upsides to the madness of the Christmas season is the incentive the big man in red provides to little kids who want to stay on their best behavior to earn the biggest booty under the tree. Savvy mothers will milk this for all it's worth.

Any mother worth her salt will exploit every birthday and holiday to get what she wants, if only for a few days.

## "You better shop around."

This nod to Smokey Robinson simply means "Don't settle for the first person you meet. Playing the field has its advantages and, besides, the longer you date, the more time I have to prepare for the wedding."

## "Calgon, take me away!"

Here's a popular expression from the '70s that women adapted from a commercial slogan. The TV spots usually depicted a stressed-out mother at the end of her rope who finds salvation, albeit temporarily, in a bubble bath. Today, moms are more likely to say "Percodan, take me away!"

Times have changed.

## "It's just  a crush, that's all."

There are few things so frightening as a teenager who remarks with more conviction than you've ever heard her muster: "I'm in love." It is then when a mother completely forgets that she was once young and in love, several times, in fact, and will try to convince the ga-ga child that she is merely infatuated.

# "You're going to leave and I'll never see you again."

This is a mother's pat response to any of the following announcements by her child:

"I've been **accepted** to college."

"I'm **joining** the **army**."

"We're getting **married**."

"I've been **transferred** to the Minneapolis office."

"We're having a **baby**."

"I'm going to **fill** the **car** up."

# "Do you have any idea what I do around here all day?"

{ This is Mom feeling unappreciated. Your answer to
this question is vital. }

### THE RIGHT ANSWER:
"Gosh, Mom, you do so many things,
I couldn't begin to list them!"

### THE WRONG ANSWER:
"Watch the soaps and eat bonbons?"

## "Don't talk to strangers!"

From the moment a child can comprehend "stranger danger," a mother will drive home the point by repeating this ism every time the poor kid leaves the house. That's why you often see kids refuse to converse with crossing guards, store clerks, traffic cops, and out-of-town uncles.

## "You get what you pay for."

Another nugget of wisdom undoubtedly learned from experience. Applies especially to furniture, hair color, and spandex undergarments.

## "That's gratitude for you."

{ Sometimes, all a mom wants is a little gratitude. Other times, Mom wants a *lot* of gratitude. It's best to err on the "more is more" side. }

## "What were you *thinking?*"

{ This is Mom's response to a child doing something incredibly stupid, such as tattooing his crush-of-the-week's name on his chest or spending a half hour in a tanning bed the day of her prom. }

# "Trends pass.
# The classics live forever."

{ This is one of those lessons in life that Mom has
learned the hard way, after spending thousands of
dollars on items like gaucho pants, go-go boots,
fringed vests, macramé vests, and Bo Derek braids. }

Listen to Mom on this one.
She's been there, bought that.

## "I'm sorry. Did I offend your delicate sensibilities?"

{ You know you're in trouble when Mom resorts to sarcasm. This is a sure sign that she is nearing her breaking point. Better act accordingly and shape up! }

## "Work? You don't know the meaning of the word!"

{ Mom's definition of the word: "**Work**: What I do all day for no pay, no pension plan, and no vacation." Kid's definition of the word: "Work: What Mom is always complaining about." }

# "Leave a little something to the imagination, would you?"

TRANSLATION:

"That halter top is smaller than my first training bra. I can't even imagine what invisible force is holding you in!"

## "When in doubt, buy the larger size."

Here's another pearl of wisdom from a mom who obviously learned this lesson the hard way. This momism particularly applies to swim suits, high heels, and maternity clothes.

## "If he loves you, he'll wait."

This ism is a classic ploy to slow things down on a daughter's runaway hormone train. The suggestion here is to play hard to get, preferably until the age of thirty.

## "I'll have one foot in the grave before I get any respect around here."

TRANSLATION:

"I'm starting to feel like Rodney Dangerfield and it's not a pretty feeling!"

## "What's so difficult about rinsing off one plate?"

This *seems* like a reasonable question. But what Mom fails to understand here is that it's not *just* the rinsing of the one plate. It's the *clearing* of the plate, and the agonizingly long walk to the kitchen where, sometimes, the sink is already crowded with *other* plates, making it *so* much easier for the child to add the plate to the stack and retreat to the TV room for a much-needed rest.

## "When do I get to meet her?"

Pity the poor mother who rarely, if ever, gets to meet her son's sweethearts. Pity more the poor son of the mother who will repeat the above ism until he relents.

## "What are you—thirteen going on thirty-three?"

This is Mom's retort when her adolescent child comes up with an uncharacteristically adult comment, such as "Vivian, pass the merlot, will you darling?"

## "If you're too sick to go to school, you're too sick to go out tonight."

Each day, around the country, children make miraculous recoveries from seemingly fatal ear infections, stomach flu, and upper respiratory ailments. Sicker than dogs at seven in the morning, they suddenly transform into pictures of health, just in time for the school dance. It's amazing, really.

## "Mommy needs some me time."

**Me time** (n.): The pursuit of a spiritual or recreational experience by oneself or in the company of like-minded adult persons. Typically sought in yoga class, bookstores, boutiques, or Chippendales floor shows.

# "I'm going to my room. Don't disturb me unless someone is bleeding to death."

{ When Mom makes this declaration, you can be sure it's a "me time" emergency. When she hangs a DO NOT DISTURB sign on her door, you know she means it. }

When she wraps her bedroom door in police tape, don't even dream of knocking!

## "You have no idea
## how easy you have it."

Nothing irks a mom faster than a child complaining how difficult his life is. Because what mom wouldn't give her eyeteeth if all she had to do was study American literature, take piano lessons, and work out in gym class every day?

## "Are you sure you want to do this?"

In the category of "Mom's Last Words," this ism is often uttered immediately before a child walks down the aisle, leaves for college, or goes under the tattoo needle.

## "Don't worry. It will grow back."

Used interchangeably for hair, eyebrows, or multi-pierced earlobes, this ism is Mom's feeble attempt to minimize a major disaster.

## "Boo-hoo.
## You're breaking my heart!"

When Mom gets *this* sarcastic, it's best to cease and desist the complaining and just take out the trash, for heaven's sake.

# "Not until you're 16 (then 18, then 21, then out of my house)."

{ Whether it pertains to body piercing, tattoos, smoking, drinking, or sex, Mom's bar tends to get higher and higher, the older the kid gets. }

## "You were too good for him (or her), anyway."

Moms are at their best when comforting a devastated child. This ism is typically used to console a teen or young adult who has been cruelly dumped by a sweetheart. It reinforces the age-old notion that nobody, but *nobody*, is going to be good enough for Mom's sweet baby.

# "He's not good enough for you, honey."

As opposed to the "You're too good for him" tact, this ism is more of a preemptive strike moms use when it's immediately apparent that her daughter has brought home a bum.

## "In a couple of weeks, you won't even remember what you were upset about."

{ When this pitiful attempt at consolation is offered to an obviously inconsolable child, chances are this ism will fall on deaf ears. But check with the same child in two weeks, and you'll find out it's true. }

## "Whatever you decide, I'll support you."

{
In an ideal world, a mom really *will* support her children no matter what they decide to do. In reality, every mom knows her support will sound much more sincere if the decision is to go to law school rather than joining a belly-dancing troupe.
}

## "I'm a mother. It's what we do."

This is Mom's stock answer to questions like:

"Why do you worry so much?"

"Why do you always have to wait up for me?"

"Why are you always bugging me?"

## "Get your feet off the table!"

In 98 out of 100 mothers, seeing feet on a table triggers an immediate physiological response including raised blood pressure, increased heart rate, and profuse perspiration. Scientists have recently identified the gene that causes this reaction and recommend that children, guests, and spouses comply with the above request, as there is no evolutionary possibility that this gene will ever disappear.

## "What do I know? I'm only the mother."

When a mother's infinite wisdom is challenged, especially by a know-it-all teenager, she will often respond with this argument-ending rhetorical question. Her strategy? By appearing to surrender, she is, in fact, reasserting her position as the mother and, therefore, the smartest person in the household.

# "No one will ever love you like your mother."

Here's a truism that's proven every day by the little things moms do for their kids—things that no one else in their right mind would do, such as:

Adding **Hershey's Kisses** to your lunch

Combing through your **hair** for lice and their **nits**

**Cleaning** out your ears

Applauding wildly after you sing
"The Way We Were," **very** badly

Blowing **kisses** on the driveway as you **leave**
for the gas station

## "Don't forget to write!"

One of the things moms fear most is losing contact with a child who's left home. This momism, or its modern-day counterpart "Don't forget to e-mail," encourages the kid to stay in touch while subtly discouraging those costly collect calls.

## "What doesn't kill us will make us stronger."

Intended as a confidence booster, these words are small comfort to a child about to plunge into the deep end of the pool for the first time in her life.

## "You're just tired, that's all."

When Mom can't come up with a rational explanation for a child's irrational behavior, like a total meltdown at the dinner table, this is often the best she can do. After all, it sounds a lot better than, "You're just an unstable, overreacting hormonal mess, that's all."

## "I wouldn't be doing this if I didn't love you so much."

{ This is what moms say as they're applying pain or punishment to a child, such as bad-tasting medicine, splinter-seeking tweezers, or a two-week grounding. The feeble attempt at justification rarely, if ever, makes the kid feel better. }

## "You'd lose your head
## if it wasn't attached."

A common criticism of a forgetful child. This from a woman who roars off from the McDonald's drive-through window without getting her change *or* her food!

# "You're breaking your father's heart."

## TRANSLATION:

"You're breaking *my* heart, but I'm too proud to admit it."

## "Don't go to any trouble."

No self-respecting mom could sleep at night knowing people went to any extra effort to make her happy, comfortable, or well fed. There's way too much guilt involved in being the center of attention.

## "It's no trouble at all."

This is Mom's standard answer to the comment "Don't go to any trouble." Even if she is preparing a five-course meal from scratch with nothing but a hot plate, she'll never admit it was a big deal.

## "Are you warm (cool) enough?"

{ In a perfect world, Mom would be able to control the personal comfort zone of every one of her friends and family with separate thermostat settings for each individual. }

Unfortunately, it's not a perfect world, which is why moms are constantly monitoring the climate with the above ism.

## "For me?!"

It's her sixtieth birthday party. Balloons and HAPPY BIRTHDAY, MOM! signs are everywhere. There are no less than five dozen guests gathered around Mom and a table is piled high with festively wrapped packages. Still, as the first gift is presented to her, she'll innocently ask the above question, her eyelashes batting and a blush coming over her cheeks, as if she is totally unaware of the attention being lavished upon her.

## "Is that too much wind on you?"

Scientific studies have shown that, within five seconds of rolling her window down in the car, a mom will pose this question to her backseat passengers. "Type A" moms will sometimes use this ism preemptively, *before* lowering the window: "Now, if this is too much wind on you, you just let me know."

## "Sleep tight.
## Don't let the bedbugs bite!"

Pity the poor kid who hears these words—uttered sweetly and reassuringly—then spends hours of lost sleep time searching his sheets with a flashlight for snaggle-toothed vermin.

## "What's wrong?!"

{ When a child comes in the house wearing anything but a beaming smile on her face, she's bound to get this frantic inquiry. }

### TRANSLATION:

"You don't look happy! Why?! Tell me now for I must set things right!"

## "When are you going to settle down and give me some grandchildren?"

Woe to the adult child who hears this for the first time, because it means that Mom's biological grandmotherly clock is off and ticking. She's already counting the days until she gets to wear that "Ask me about my grandchildren" T-shirt.

## "You're skin and bones.
## What are they feeding you?"

Heaven help the kid who goes away to camp, college, or the military and loses a little weight around the middle. Now Mom will make it Priority One to fatten up her wayward child who is wasting away.

## "There are no small parts, only small actors."

 This is what Mom says to console a child who didn't land the lead in the school play.

NOTE:
This one is not to be used when the child's assigned role is "Munchkin No. 5" in *The Wizard of Oz.*

## "That's the way the cookie crumbles."

{ The crumbling cookie analogy usually refers to those "You win some, you lose some" scenarios, although it can be applied to beginner baking sessions. }

## "I'm damned if I do and damned if I don't."

{ The ultimate expression of maternal remorse, this ism reflects the frustration embedded in every decision a mother makes in her entire life. It means "Whatever I decide, the kid is still going to complain to his therapist one day that it was all my fault. And they'll probably be right." }

## "I'm not getting any younger, you know."

Mostly uttered when Mom gets tired of waiting for something like a wedding, grandchildren, or her turn to use the phone.

## "Welcome to *my* world."

In this case, Mom's world means the universe of nonstop work where no achievement or task is truly appreciated, a world where worry is the order of the day and guilt, the dessert. A world of endless diets, fruitless exercise regimens, and carpool chaos. It is not a welcoming place, but misery loves company and moms are more than happy to share the grief.

## "It's the easiest pain to forget."

{ This ism refers to the pain of labor and delivery and is meant to quell a daughter's fear of childbirth. }

It is a bold-faced lie, of course. But, as every mother knows, if we told the truth, the human race would come to an end.

# "I'm at my wits' end!"

_____
TRANSLATION:
_____

"I am so stressed out, I have lost my wits. I can no longer find anything you say or do witty, and I seriously doubt I will rediscover my wits in the next twenty-four hours. Everyone within two miles of me would do well to stay clear until my wits return, wherever they are."

## "I gave up a career on the stage for this?!"

Usually muttered under her breath while folding her ninth load of laundry or cleaning up after a sick child, this ism conveniently ignores the fact that mom's so-called stage career ended after that unfortunate accident in the ninth grade talent show.

## "I am not your personal secretary!"

This is what Mom says when she realizes, to her utter dismay, that her weekly planner lists more appointments for her kids than it does for herself.

## "It's just a phase; you'll grow out of it."

Three parts wishful thinking and one part mother's wisdom, this ism is used to comfort the child who finds himself with an annoying developmental glitch like boney knees or a squeaky pubescent voice.

## "That's the price we pay for being a woman."

This cryptic quip is typically an earnest but somewhat misguided attempt to weigh in on the biological disadvantages of being female—namely cramps, labor pains, and hot flashes.

## "See? Isn't this fun?"

Ever the cheerleader, moms are determined to show kids a good time, especially during those dreaded extended visits to the grandparents or the Museum of Colonial Costumes.

This one is usually met with blank zombie-like stares from the kids.

## "Into each life
## a little rain must fall."

When a mom waxes poetic about life and rain, you know she has finally run out of original material.

## "I've had it up to here."

Pay close attention to Mom's body language when she makes this exclamation. If she indicates "here" as anywhere above her head, that means she's about to explode. Evacuate the premises immediately!

# "Absence makes the heart grow fonder."

{ This is what Mom says to a distraught, lovesick daughter when her older boyfriend—the one driving the fast convertible with the leopard skin interior and mega subwoofer—packs up and leaves for college. }

What she really means: "Good riddance!"

# "You're giving me gray hairs!"

TRANSLATION:

"By constantly worrying about you, day and night,
I have aged at four times the normal human rate
and am now the physiological equivalent of my
deceased grandmother."

## "I don't want any presents. The pleasure of your company is enough."

{ This ism is Mom's noble attempt to de-emphasize the importance of material possessions, particularly Mother's Day or birthday gifts. }

Don't believe her for a minute!

## "End of discussion."

This is what Mom says when she realizes she is losing an argument with a formidable opponent, such as her teenage son, who is passionately promoting the educational advantages of owning his own laptop computer.

## "Cleanliness is next to godliness."

Cleanliness is very important to mothers. Clean is a reflection that everything is good in her world. When her house and children are clean, especially at the same time, it truly can be a spiritual experience for which some mothers actually get down on their knees and pray in gratitude.

## "It's nothing that a good meal can't fix."

{ Sometimes, when a mom can't think of another way to soothe a child's aching heart or body, she turns to the guaranteed universal cure-all: food. }

---

TRANSLATION:

"Nothing I'm going to say will make you feel better, so how about a nice pork chop?"

**"Remember, whenever you point
your finger at someone else, most
of your fingers still point back at you."**

This somewhat confusing ism is commonly used
after one child has accused another child of causing
an accident, such as a broken window or smashed
vase, while engaging in horseplay.

More simply stated it means "You're both grounded!"

# "You were the best, by far."

Let's face it. When it comes to their kids, moms aren't exactly the most objective critics. That's why no matter how badly a child performs in a school play, dance recital, or debate, Mom will whisper this in her young one's ear as soon as the performance is over . . . even as the kid is being pelted with rotten tomatoes.

## "Sleep on it, then decide."

Kids are impulsive creatures. They want what they want, and they want it *now*. This ism is Mom's way of delaying those life-altering decisions like whether or not to get a tattoo, tongue piercing, or shocking pink streaks in their hair.

## "I love you."

No translation necessary.